KU-017-738

# Contents

# A day at the fair

Can you find:

Balancing?

Floating?

Pushing?

Sliding?

2

# Pushes and pulls: weight

What do you think is going on in these pictures?

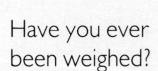

Have you ever been weighed?

Children and babies are weighed to make sure that they are putting on weight and growing properly.

4

Many grown-ups in Britain weigh themselves to make sure that they are not putting on too much weight.

Shopkeepers have scales to weigh fruit and vegetables.

Can you think of other people who use weighing scales?

# Keeping safe near water

Before you learn to swim you should
wear something which will help you
to float when you go in the water.

You could wear ▲
armbands like these
or you might wear
a safety jacket.  ➤

These will help
you keep afloat
in the water.

**Rafts**

**Life jackets**

**Life boats**

**Inflatable life boats**

**Rings**

Just in case this ferry boat sinks it has lots of things on board which help people to float.

These will all help to keep people safe until they can be rescued.

Remember that water can be very dangerous. You should always keep away from the edge.

# What floats? What sinks?

This boat is floating.

Why is this boat sinking?

Marsha and Stuart are floating on the lilo.
What happened to them?

What do you think happened to the bucket and the hat when they fell in the water?

# Getting around

How do these children keep moving?

How do you think these children can stop moving?

What are some of the different ways
which you use to get around?

# Going to Pakistan

A few weeks ago, my Dad told me that
now I am seven, I can go with them on
their next trip to see my grandparents in
Pakistan. I was so excited. I started
planning all the things I was going to
take with me. There was so much I
wanted to show them – toys, books and
some of my new clothes.

Mum bought me a new suitcase with
wheels at the back.
'Don't pack in too much,' she said,
'because you have to be able to carry
that all by yourself.'
'That's OK – it's got wheels, it will
be easy to move it.'

At last the day came and we were ready
to go to the airport. First, I had to get the
case downstairs. I nearly fell down the
stairs, it was so heavy – you can't use
wheels on the stairs.
We got a taxi to the underground station.

More stairs led to the escalator!
But at least I didn't have to carry it
down the escalator.

At the airport, we found a trolley
and we piled all the cases up on it.
That made life easier!

We had to check in our cases so that
they could be loaded onto the plane.
We had to lift all the cases onto the scales.
First they were weighed, then they
went on a moving belt to where they
would be loaded.

People at the other end lifted them onto
trucks to drive them to the plane.
There they used a special conveyor
belt to load them on the plane.

I thought those wheels on my case were
going to be really useful for moving my
case but I hardly used them. I sat on the
plane thinking about all the different
ways my case was moved.

How many can you remember?

# How many ways can you move?

You can bend over to touch your toes.

You can stretch up tall, making yourself look really straight.

You can curl your body into a round shape.

14

You can lift one leg at a time.

You may be able to push your head between your legs.

You can make shapes with your body.

**Wow!**

Did you know that there are 206 bones in your body?

# STOP!

How are these children stopping their bikes?

We can stop things moving in many different ways.

Can you think of any other ways to stop things moving?

# Making things easier to lift

This bundle is very difficult to carry.
It is much easier with a handle.

If you have to carry
something heavy,
it is often easier to
carry it on your back.

**Wow!**

You can't lift your mum like this:

*groan!!*

But you can lift her if you sit on the see-saw like this:

*easy!!*

Have you ever tried to lift one of your friends up?

If you both sit on a see-saw it is much easier.

You can take it in turns to lift each other up.

# Animal movement

These animals have a smooth shape so they can move through water or air quickly.

Swallows fly all the way from Africa to Britain each summer. They return to Africa in the autumn.

Cheetahs live in Africa. They can run at over 100 kilometres per hour – but only for a short time.

Dolphins can jump right out of the water. They can swim at 40 kilometres per hour!

Can you guess which animals these skeletons belong to?

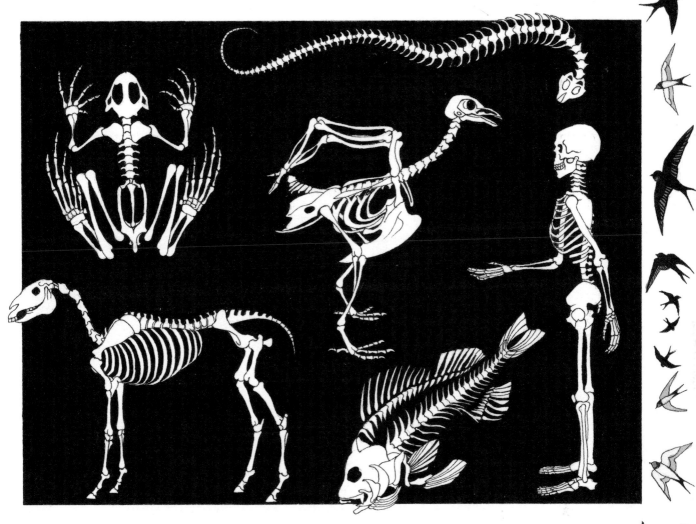

Which of the animals do you think is good at:

Jumping    Running    Flying    Sliding    Swimming

# Getting dressed

What pushes and pulls do you do
when you get dressed?

# Index